What Is the Story of Wonder Woman™?

What Is the Story of Wonder Woman™?

by Steve Korté

illustrated by Jake Murray

Penguin Workshop

For Bill—SK

For Krysti—JM

PENGUIN WORKSHOP
An Imprint of Penguin Random House LLC, New York

Wonder Woman created by William Moulton Marston

Published by Penguin Workshop, an imprint of Penguin Random House LLC, New York. PENGUIN and PENGUIN WORKSHOP are trademarks of Penguin Books Ltd. WHO HQ & Design is a registered trademark of Penguin Random House LLC. Printed in the USA.

Visit us online at www.penguinrandomhouse.com.

Library of Congress Cataloging-in-Publication Data is available upon request.

ISBN 9781524788278 (paperback)   10 9 8 7 6 5 4 3 2
ISBN 9781524788285 (library binding)   10 9 8 7 6 5 4 3 2 1

Contents

What Is the Story of Wonder Woman? 1

To Tell the Truth 4

The Birth of Comic Books 18

Here Come the Heroes 24

An Amazing Idea 35

A Dazzling Debut 44

Challenges 56

Hard Times for Heroes 64

Wonder Woman Triumphant 69

Wonder Woman Goes to the Movies 90

Bibliography 106

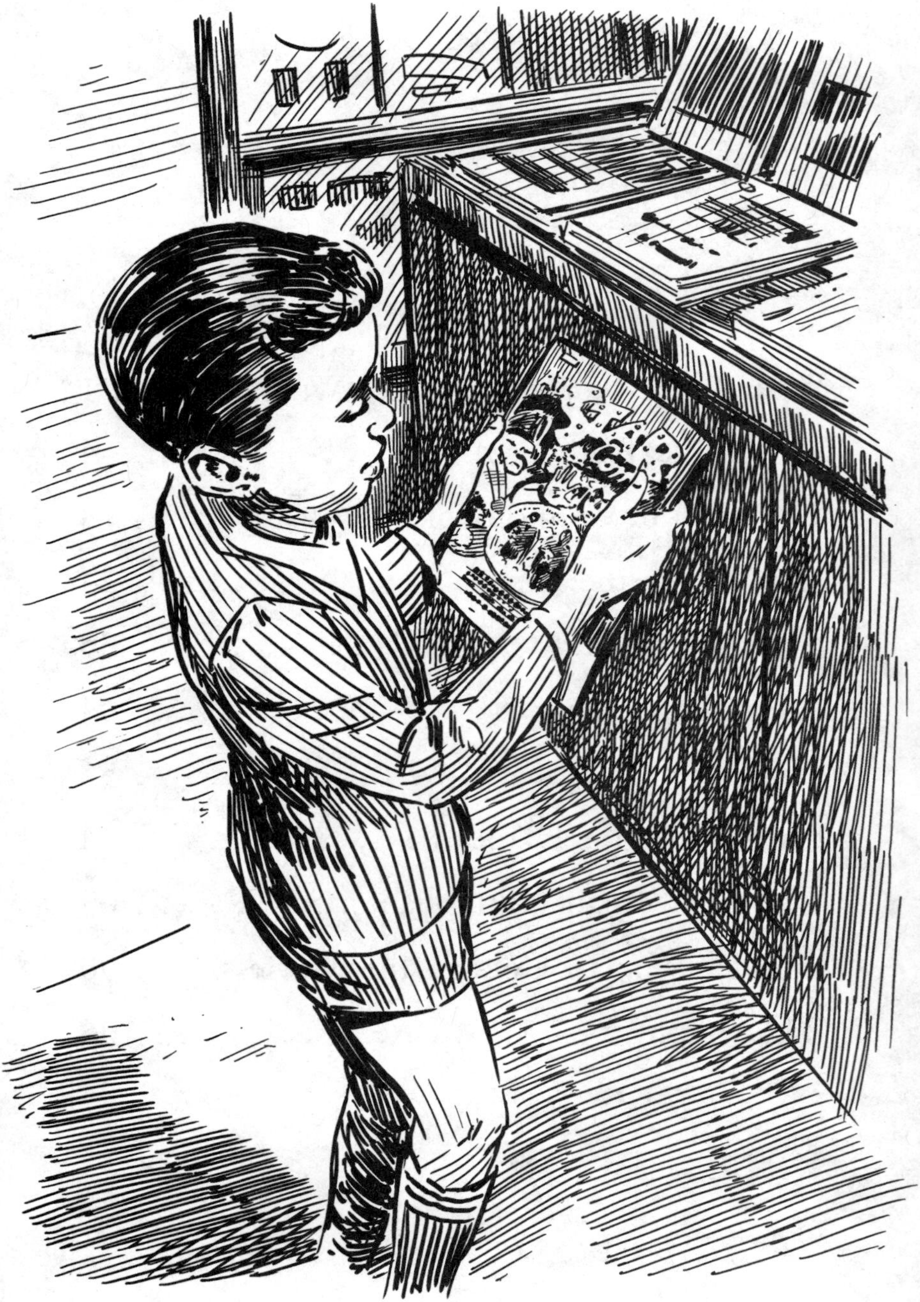

What Is the Story of Wonder Woman?

On October 21, 1941, issue number eight of a comic book called *All-Star Comics* hit the newsstands and stores in America. It contained an exciting story starring the super hero team known as the Justice Society of America. Superman and Batman were members of the team. But this story featured other heroes—including Hawkman, Dr. Fate, Johnny Thunder, Sandman, Starman, Doctor Mid-Nite, and an owl named Hooty— who joined forces to fight a criminal mastermind known as Professor Elba.

Within the back pages of this same issue was a shorter story featuring the debut of another super hero. But this was a super hero like no other in comic history. In a time when nearly every comic book hero was a man, this hero's name was

Wonder Woman. And that's not all that made her unique. The background history of the character— her origin story—was inspired by Greek and Roman myths that have been around for thousands of years. In this first story she was compared to gods and goddesses: "As lovely as Aphrodite—as wise as Athena—with the speed of Mercury and the strength of Hercules." Her mother was the queen of the Amazons, a tribe of strong warrior women who lived on Paradise Island, where no men were allowed. Wonder Woman was the strongest and bravest of all the Amazons!

By the end of the story, this Amazing Amazon was ready to leave Paradise Island so that she could save America—and the rest of the world—from disaster. The story of Wonder Woman had begun!

Mercury, the Roman messenger of the gods,
and Athena, the Greek goddess of wisdom

CHAPTER 1
To Tell the Truth

Like almost every other comic book super hero, Wonder Woman had a secret identity. On Paradise Island, she was known as Princess Diana, the daughter of the queen of the Amazons. In America, her secret identity was a nurse named Diana Prince.

What few people knew, though, was that the man who wrote the Wonder Woman comics had a secret identity of his own. In the earliest stories, he was credited as "Charles Moulton." But that was not his real name.

William Moulton Marston—called Bill by his family and friends—was the man who created Wonder Woman. But that was just one of his many accomplishments. He was also a lawyer,

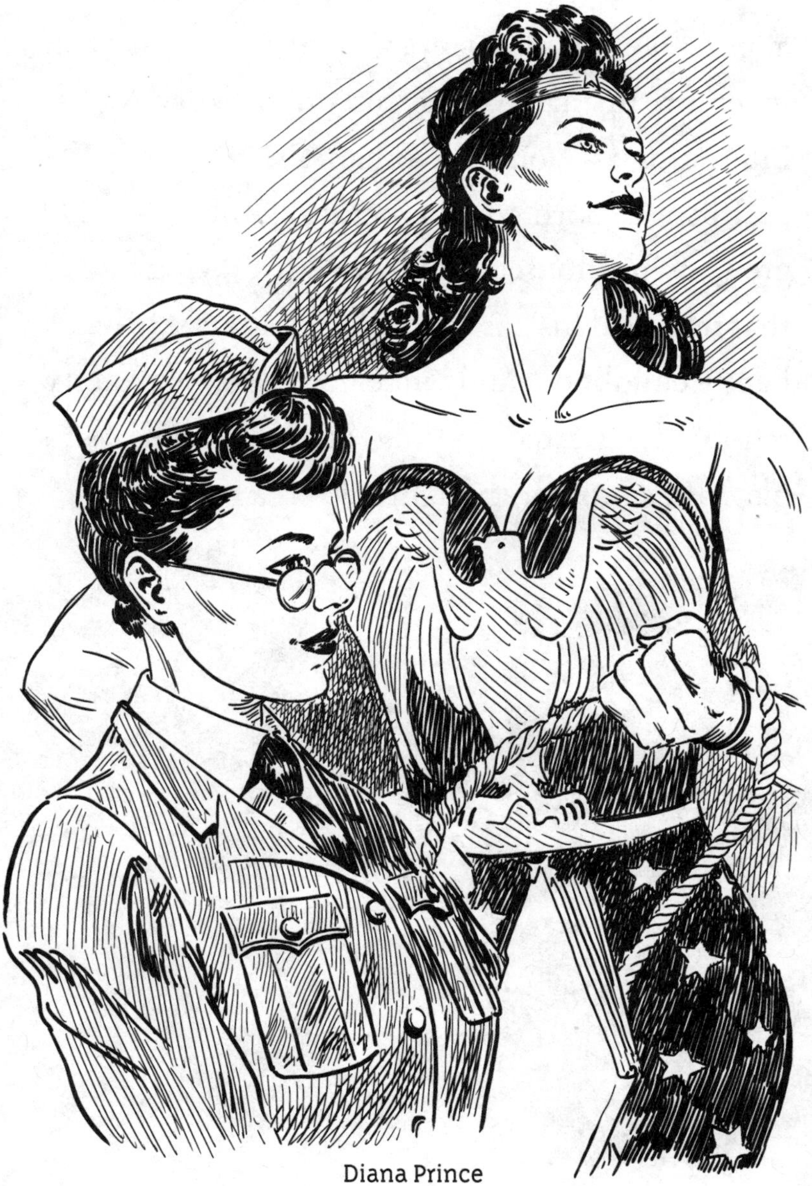

Diana Prince

a psychologist, a scientist, a professor, and an inventor. In many ways, his origin story was as interesting as Wonder Woman's!

Bill was born in Massachusetts in 1893. He grew up in a household filled with a loving family that included his parents and four aunts. He had a happy childhood, and while he was in elementary school, he started writing stories, poems, and plays. His mother thought he was a genius.

By the time he entered high school, Bill had grown tall and handsome. He excelled in his classes, played football, and was elected class president. Early on, he developed an interest in Greek history and mythology. In high school, he wrote a class paper that was an imaginary conversation between himself and Clio, the Greek goddess of history.

Clio, the Greek goddess of history

Since the eighth grade, Bill had been in love with a girl named Elizabeth Holloway. One of the things he admired about Elizabeth was that she was not shy about expressing her opinions. When

Bill and Elizabeth graduated from high school, he applied to Harvard. On his college application, Bill was asked to fill in his "intended occupation." He wrote one word: "law."

In 1911, Harvard did not admit women as students, so Elizabeth applied to Mount Holyoke College, one of the first women's colleges in the United States. Elizabeth shared Bill's interest in Greek history. Her favorite book was written by the poet Sappho, who lived in Greece around 600 BC. Elizabeth was even able to read Sappho's writing in the original Greek! In the years to come, Bill and Elizabeth's love of Greek literature played an important part in the creation of the character of Wonder Woman.

Sappho

Bill did very well in his classes at Harvard. He still hoped to become a lawyer, but he was soon drawn to the school's Department of Psychology, where students studied the science of human behavior. Bill and one of his professors were interested in the study of deception—the act of telling a lie. The two men wanted to be able to learn for certain if a person was telling the truth or not.

Bill began experimenting to invent a machine that could tell truth from lies. One of his ideas was to see if a person's blood pressure changed when he or she told a lie. Bill tested a large group of students by monitoring changes in their blood pressure as each student told a truth and then a lie. Out of 107 tests, Bill was able to tell a truthful statement from a lie 103 times, or 96 percent of the time, just by watching and recording someone's blood pressure!

Bill Marston created his lie detector test in

1914, but he chose not to patent his idea. The patent would have required others to pay Bill each time the test was used. In his book *The Lie Detector Test*, he wrote that important scientific discoveries should be free for all to use. That decision would end up costing Bill a lot of money in the years to come.

The Lie Detector

In 1931, a man named Leonarde Keeler patented a lie detector machine that he called the Keeler polygraph. Like Bill Marston's machine, Keeler's recorded changes in blood pressure. But the new machine also measured a person's pulse, changes in perspiration, and rate of breathing. These additional measurements made the Keeler polygraph even more reliable than Bill's machine. The lie detector machine used today is very similar to the Keeler polygraph.

Bill and Elizabeth graduated from college in 1915 and got married soon after that. Even though Bill was still interested in science, both he and Elizabeth decided to pursue law degrees. Bill enrolled in Harvard Law School.

Elizabeth later recalled, "Those dumb bunnies at Harvard wouldn't take women, so I went to Boston University."

In the United States in 1915, women did not have many of the same rights as men. Women were not allowed to vote in many states. Bill and Elizabeth joined the fight, known as women's suffrage, to change this inequality. Bill was fond of saying that he believed that women should rule the world because he thought women understood love better than men. And love, he declared, was more powerful than any man's physical strength.

The Women's Suffrage Movement

The word *suffrage* means "the right to vote."

In the late 1800s, many people opposed women's suffrage because they actually believed that women were less intelligent than men! Some people feared that families would suffer if women began to vote or got involved in politics in any way. It wasn't until 1920 that the Nineteenth Amendment was added to the US Constitution, giving women the right to vote.

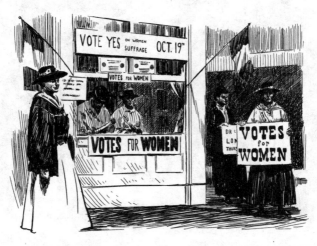

Bill and Elizabeth both graduated from law school, but neither one ever practiced law. At the time, fewer than 2 percent of all lawyers in the United States were women. Elizabeth found small jobs where she could. Bill started teaching at Tufts University in Massachusetts. More than anything else, though, he hoped that he would become famous for his lie detector.

CHAPTER 2
The Birth of Comic Books

The Marston family grew to include four children. Like most kids in the 1930s, they loved to read comic books. Each week, they would read and trade dozens of new titles. Comic books had arrived in the early 1930s. Before comic books came along, there were small, inexpensive magazines filled with detective and adventure stories. They were called pulp magazines. The pulps were very popular with young readers, especially boys.

Pulp Magazines

Paper is made from wood chips that are mashed into a soupy base called pulp. The pulp is then processed into a mat that is heated, rolled, and compressed into paper. Pulp magazines were printed on cheap, rough-textured paper that was closer to the actual pulpy base than to fine, smooth paper. More respectable magazines, such as *Ladies' Home Journal* and the *Saturday Evening Post*, were printed on expensive paper that was slick and glossy.

Pulp magazines were published from the late 1800s until the 1950s. They were especially popular in the 1920s and 1930s. Costing less than twenty-five cents, they sometimes sold up to one million copies a week!

Comic strips had been appearing in newspapers since the 1890s, but the first person to collect comics into a magazine—or a comic book—was Max Gaines. In 1933, he released *Famous Funnies: A Carnival of Comics*, which most historians consider the first true American comic book. There was no cover price on that issue, but the second issue sold for ten cents. Soon that became the standard price for all comic books. Most children could afford to buy them, and by the late 1930s, comic books became a big business.

Max Gaines (1894–1947)

Maxwell Charles Gaines got his start in business working as a salesman for a printing press. In 1933, he created the first four-color newsprint pamphlet—the original comic book format. Five years after launching 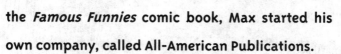 the *Famous Funnies* comic book, Max started his own company, called All-American Publications.

Max sold his company to DC Comics in 1944 and went on to form Educational Comics (known as EC). His son William "Bill" Gaines headed EC Comics after Max's death, publishing *MAD* magazine and a line of horror comics that included *Tales from the Crypt*.

Max Gaines is remembered as "the father of American comic books."

Famous Funnies and most of the earliest comic books were filled with reprinted comic strips from the Sunday newspapers. But there was one man who had an idea for a new type of comic book. His name was Major Malcolm Wheeler-Nicholson, and he was a pulp magazine writer and

former cavalry officer. He formed a company in New York City called National Allied Publications and, in 1935, published *New Fun: The Big Comic*

Magazine. New Fun was bigger than *Famous Funnies*, measuring ten by fifteen inches. And it contained brand-new, all original stories.

New Fun was not very successful, but the major managed to launch a few more titles, including *Detective Comics*. Eventually, National Allied Publications was sold to new owners. Within a few years, the company would become known as DC Comics. And thanks to one *very* famous super hero, DC Comics became the most successful comic book company in the world.

CHAPTER 3
Here Come the Heroes

Around the same time that Major Wheeler-Nicholson was getting ready to publish *New Fun*, two teenagers from Cleveland had a new comic idea. Writer Jerry Siegel and artist Joe Shuster were the very best of friends, and together they created the character of a man from outer space. He wore a costume of, as Joe put it, "the brightest colors we could think of." He had amazing powers, including super strength and the ability to leap tall buildings in a single bound. And he used his powers to fight crime. They called him Superman.

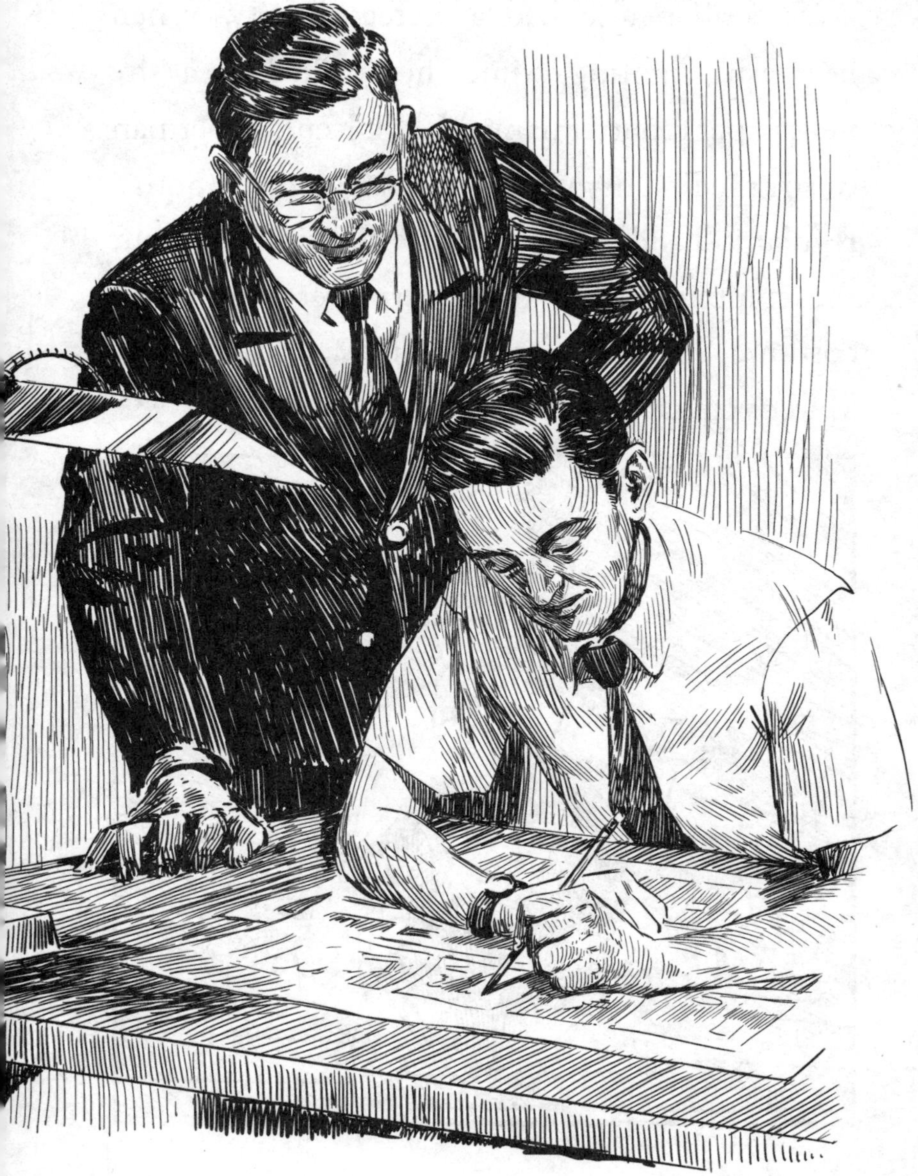

Superman also had a secret identity. When he wasn't fighting crime, he worked as a shy newspaper reporter named Clark Kent. Superman wasn't the first hero to have a dual identity (both a regular job and a hidden crime-fighting one), but the combination of his superpowers, his flashy costume, *and* his secret identity created a new kind of character: the super hero.

More than anything else, Jerry and Joe wanted their new super hero to star in his own newspaper comic strip, but every publisher in the United States turned down the two teens. Four years later, Max Gaines came across the sample Superman newspaper strips that Jerry and Joe had created. He knew that DC Comics was looking for a new story to include in the very first issue of a comic book they were about to launch.

Jerry, Joe, and DC made a deal. And in 1938, Superman soared through the sky in *Action Comics* #1.

No one expected Superman to be a hit, but he turned out to be the most successful and imitated idea in comic books. Suddenly, comics started selling in very big numbers—close to a million copies a month for the most popular titles! More costumed super heroes soon arrived. Batman made his debut in *Detective Comics* in 1939, and he was also a big hit with readers.

DC and other publishers introduced dozens of other super heroes, including Shazam (then known as Captain Marvel), The Flash, and Green Lantern. Kids quickly fell in love with comic books, but at the same time, some adults started to wonder if comics were good for children.

Some parents and psychologists were worried about the violence in comic books. Superman usually beat up the villains in his stories. In a few of his earliest adventures, Batman even carried a gun!

On May 8, 1940, the *Chicago Daily News* published an angry article about the harmful effects of comic books on children, saying "Unless we want a coming generation even more ferocious than the present one, parents and teachers throughout America must band together to break the 'comic' magazine."

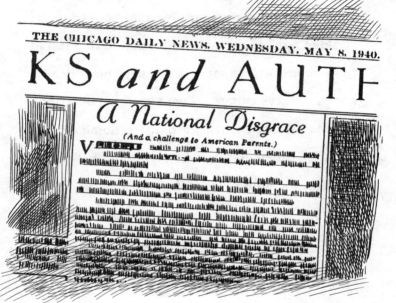

Comic books were suddenly under attack. DC Comics instituted a new policy: None of their heroes would kill anyone. The new approach meant that memorable villains could return again and again in the DC comic stories.

Comic Book Villains

Every super hero needs a worthy foe to battle. Many famous super-villains were introduced in the "Golden Age" of comic books, a period that lasted from about 1938 to 1955. Superman's most deadly enemy was Lex Luthor, whom Superman described as "the mad scientist who plots to dominate the earth." Batman had a whole rogues' gallery of villains, including the Joker, Catwoman, Two-Face, and the Penguin. Shazam battled one of the strangest villains in comics: Mister Mind, a super-intelligent two-inch worm from another planet.

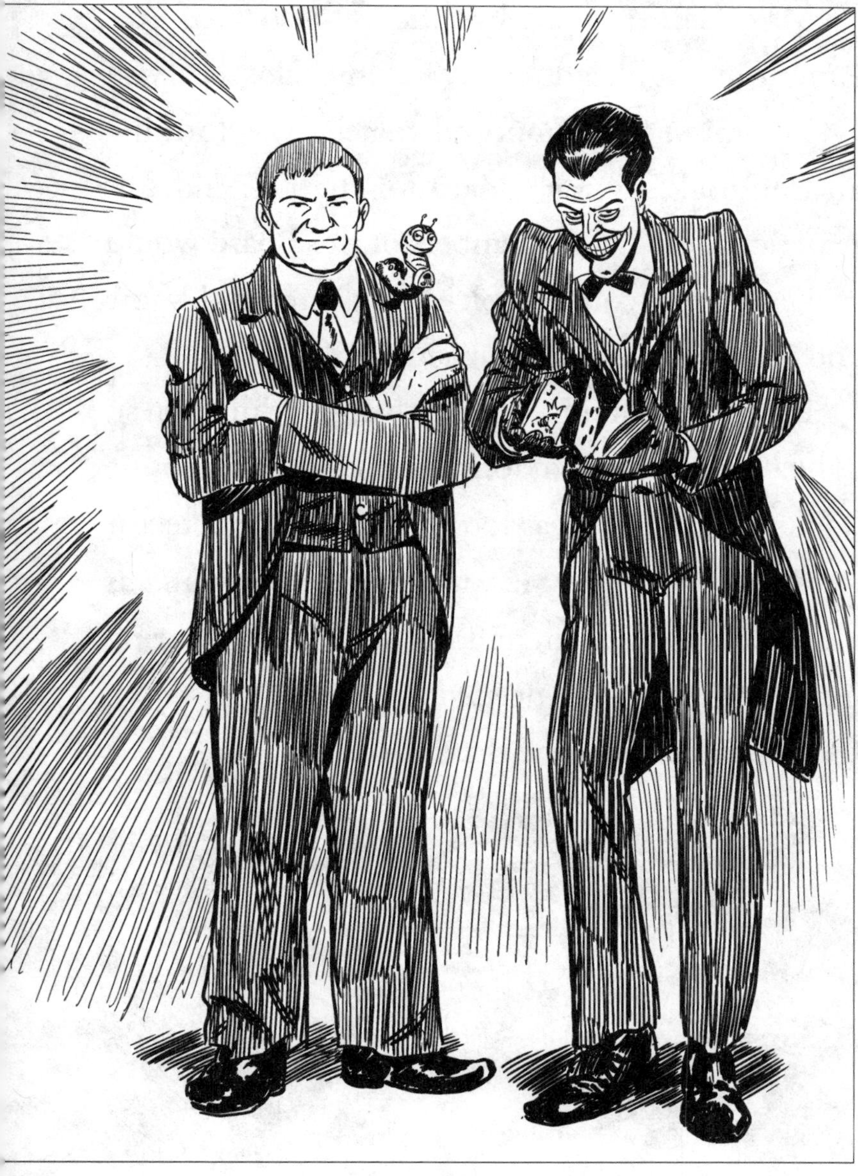

Max Gaines was now the publisher of All-American Publications. Working closely with DC Comics, he announced that he was forming an Editorial Advisory Board for the DC and All-American lines. The members of this board would make sure that comic book stories were wholesome and promoted good citizenship.

Bill Marston noticed these changes with interest, as he watched his own four children reading comic books. His many ideas to promote the lie detector test had fizzled out. He was no longer working as a university professor, and his writing didn't bring in much money. Bill needed an idea for a new job. Could comic books be the answer?

CHAPTER 4
An Amazing Idea

At the Marston home in Massachusetts, Bill and Elizabeth lived with their children and Olive Byrne, one of Bill's former students at Tufts University. Elizabeth traveled to New York City every day to go to work, and Olive stayed at home to care for the children.

Olive Byrne

In 1935, Olive started working as a staff writer for *Family Circle*, a popular weekly women's magazine. She contributed articles to the magazine, writing under the name "Olive Richard." In her first story, she wrote about a young boy who was a nonstop liar. Olive decided to investigate a device she had heard about: a lie detector machine. In *Family Circle* she wrote, "So I made up my mind to meet the man who invented it—Dr. William Moulton Marston, psychologist and lawyer. I arrived at his large rambling house set high on a hill." Although she lived in this very house with Bill and his family, Olive pretended that she had never even met him before!

Olive wrote many more stories for *Family Circle*, and she interviewed Bill in most of them. This gave Bill the opportunity to offer advice on a wide variety of topics, including dating tips for young girls and ideas on how to save a failing marriage.

In an issue dated October 25, 1940, Olive tackled the issue of comic book violence. She interviewed Bill for an article called "Don't Laugh at the Comics."

In her article, Olive wrote, "I know from observation in my own household that children read the so-called funnies morning, noon, and—unfortunately—night." She asked Bill for reassurance that comics were, in fact, good for kids.

Children read the so-called funnies morning, noon, and - unfortunately - night.

Bill replied that there were about 108 comic books on newsstands, reaching forty to fifty million readers every month. He had been doing research on comics for more than a year. Amazingly, he had read almost every comic book published during that time!

Bill also paid a compliment to Max Gaines, saying that Gaines understood what appeals to the emotions of young readers.

In New York City, Max Gaines read Olive's article and decided that Bill Marston was just the man to join his Editorial Advisory Board. Bill happily accepted the new position, and he asked Max if they could set up a meeting. Bill had something much bigger in mind than a board position.

When they got together, Bill told Max that he wanted to write stories for comic books. He had an idea for a new hero, but this one would be different from all the others. This would be a

female super hero: Suprema the Wonder Woman!

Max wasn't sure that was a good idea. In the early days of comics, it was assumed that most of their readers were young boys, and Max didn't think that a female super hero comic would appeal to boys. Bill strongly disagreed.

Bill wanted "to create a feminine character with all the strength of Superman," who was also "a good and beautiful woman."

Bill even argued that having a female hero would double sales by appealing to boys *and* girls!

The Greek Influence

Bill Marston filled his Wonder Woman stories with gods and goddesses from Greek mythology. The mighty god Zeus ruled over all of them from the top of Mount Olympus. Aphrodite was the goddess of love and beauty, and Athena was the goddess of wisdom and war. Hercules was the son of Zeus, and he was one of the strongest men on Earth. A few Roman gods also made appearances, including Mercury, who was the messenger of the gods. Mercury could run faster than any other Roman god.

Zeus

Max decided to give it a try. In 1941, Bill submitted a typewritten story featuring the debut of "Suprema the Wonder Woman." It was about gods and goddesses from ancient Greek mythology, and it featured a tribe of powerful women known as the Amazons.

Bill decided to use the name "Charles Moulton" for his first Wonder Woman story. Charles was Max's middle name, and Moulton was Bill's.

After he submitted his story, Bill asked to be consulted if any edits were necessary. He wrote, "I hope you'll call me up about any changes in the story, names, costumes, or subject matter." His editor, Sheldon Mayer, made one big change. He removed "Suprema" from the main character's name. Wonder Woman first appeared in *All-Star Comics* #8 in 1941.

Early Super Heroines

A heroine is a woman who is admired for her courage and achievements. Wonder Woman was not the first costumed heroine to appear in comic books. Some of the others who preceded her had superpowers, and some did not. Phantom Lady, who arrived in 1941, only a few months before Wonder Woman, used a device called a "black-light projector" to blind her enemies and make herself invisible. Two other 1941 heroines were the super-strong Miss Victory in a red, white, and blue uniform, and Bulletgirl, who wore a bullet-shaped helmet that allowed her to fly. A few years earlier, a 1937 British magazine called *Wags* introduced the powerful heroine Sheena, Queen of the Jungle, who wore a leopard-skin outfit and had a monkey sidekick named Chim.

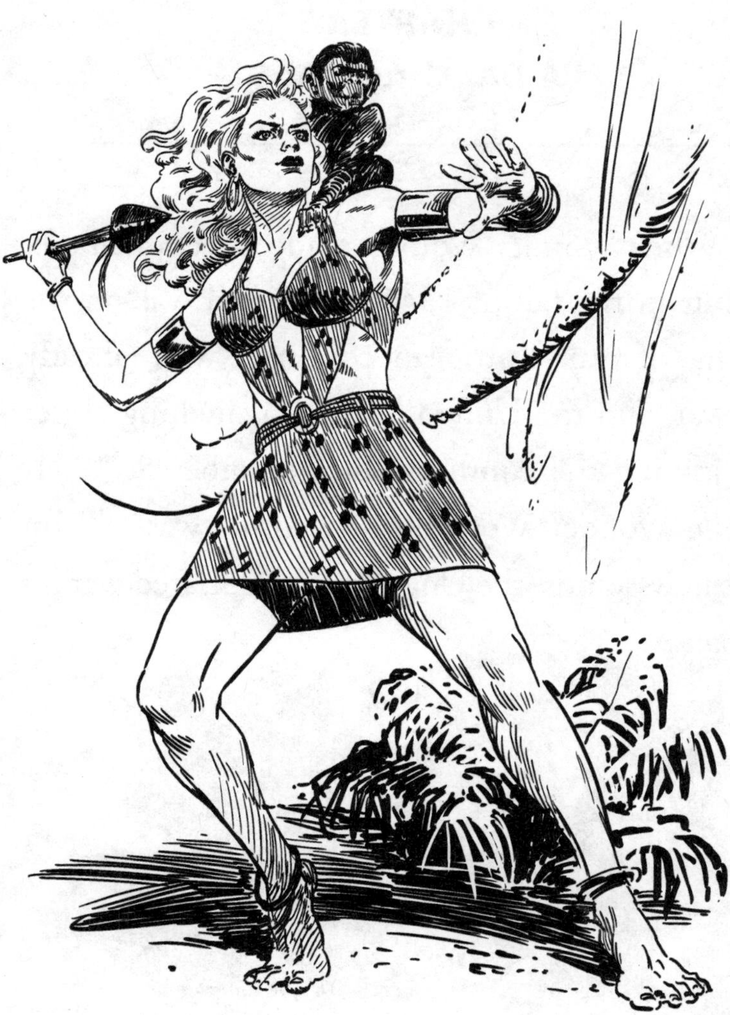

Sheena and Chim

CHAPTER 5
A Dazzling Debut

When Wonder Woman made her comic book debut in the fall of 1941, the world was on the brink of war. European countries were already at war, and the United States was inching closer to joining the conflict. On December 8, 1941, while Wonder Woman's first comic was still on the newsstands, the United States declared war on Japan.

US president Franklin D. Roosevelt, December 1941

Bill Marston did not join the military, but in Wonder Woman he created the perfect patriotic hero. She left her home—a mysterious island in the middle of the ocean—and traveled to America in order to fight for truth and justice. Wonder Woman's outfit was the same colors as the flag of the United States. She wore a star-spangled skirt, a red blouse with yellow eagle wings on its front, and red boots. The artist who designed her outfit was Harry George Peter.

H. G. Peter (1880–1958)

The first artist to draw Wonder Woman was Harry George Peter—known as "H. G." As a young man, he drew newspaper illustrations for the *San Francisco Chronicle.* Like Bill Marston, he believed in the importance of women's suffrage.

His first comic illustrations were for Funnies, Inc., where he drew the super hero called Man o' Metal. Harry was sixty-one years old when he started working on Wonder Woman, and he would continue to draw her stories for nearly the next two decades. He is most famous for creating the lasting image of Wonder Woman in 1941.

Here is how Bill introduced Wonder Woman in her first story: "With a hundred times the agility and strength of our best male athletes and strongest wrestlers, she appears as though from nowhere to avenge an injustice or right a wrong! As lovely as Aphrodite—as wise as Athena—with the speed of Mercury and the strength of Hercules, she is known only as Wonder Woman. But who she is, or whence she came, nobody knows!"

Wonder Woman came from Paradise Island, home to a race of warrior women known as the Amazons. The Amazons were immortal—that meant they lived forever. They were led by the brave Queen Hippolyte, and they remained happily hidden from the rest of the world. In fact, no man had ever appeared on their island. That changed when an American army pilot named Steve Trevor crashed onto Paradise Island.

Queen Hippolyte was very upset to learn that her very own daughter, Diana, had fallen in love with the injured pilot. Hippolyte decided to ask the goddesses Aphrodite and Athena what she should do about this problem. They told the queen that America needed her help. Hippolyte was instructed to choose one brave Amazon to accompany Steve Trevor back to America.

"I shall find the strongest and wisest of the Amazons," declared Hippolyte. "She shall go forth to fight for liberty and freedom and all womankind."

The queen then set up a series of difficult athletic contests to choose her Amazon champion. The most unusual event was "bullets and bracelets," where two Amazon women faced each other with guns.

"Each of you will shoot five times," explained Hippolyte. "Your opponent must catch the bullets on her bracelet—or else expect to be wounded!"

The winner of the contest was a masked Amazon who turned out to be Princess Diana, the queen's daughter.

Hippolyte presented Diana with a costume she designed herself. The queen told her daughter, "In America you'll indeed be a 'Wonder Woman.'"

Bill ended the story with these words: "And so Diana, the Wonder Woman, giving up her heritage, and her right to eternal life, leaves Paradise Island to take the man she loves back to America—the land she learns to love and protect, and adopts as her own!"

Readers quickly fell in love with Wonder Woman. She had it all: power, great intelligence, and beauty. She also created a secret identity in the United States. She put on a pair of glasses and pretended to be a nurse named Diana Prince, who worked at the Walter Reed Army Hospital.

Steve Trevor quickly recovered from his injuries and declared his love for Wonder Woman. He

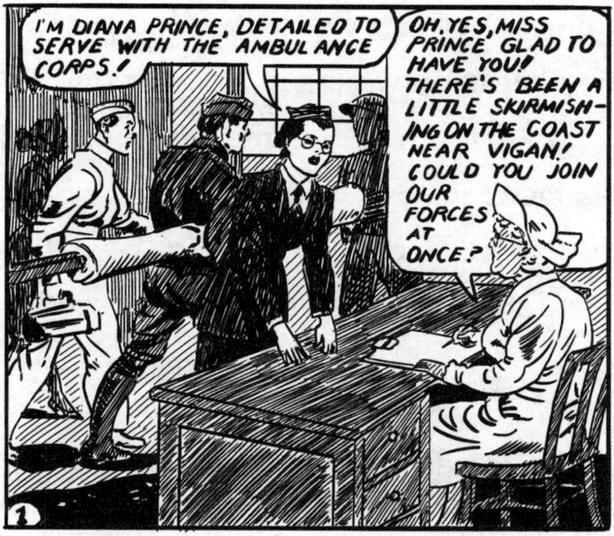
I'M DIANA PRINCE, DETAILED TO SERVE WITH THE AMBULANCE CORPS!
OH, YES, MISS PRINCE GLAD TO HAVE YOU! THERE'S BEEN A LITTLE SKIRMISHING ON THE COAST NEAR VIGAN! COULD YOU JOIN OUR FORCES AT ONCE?

called her his "beautiful angel" and asked her to marry him. She turned him down, explaining that she couldn't marry anyone until she had eliminated crime and injustice on Earth.

Sadly, Steve was less impressed with Diana Prince. One time he said to her, "Listen, Diana! You're a nice kid, and I like you. But if you think you can hold a candle to Wonder Woman you're crazy!" Crazy or not, Diana decided to give up her nursing job and become Steve's secretary.

Wonder Woman's comics were so popular that she soon began appearing in titles beyond *All-Star Comics*. In 1942, she became the cover star and lead character in *Sensation Comics*. That same year, she earned her very own *Wonder Woman* comic book, and she joined The Flash and Green Lantern in *Comic Cavalcade*.

Millions of copies of her comics were sold each month. And the actual number of readers was even higher, as most kids shared their comics with others.

As her stories multiplied, she acquired some wonderful devices, including an Invisible Airplane (later it became a jet), a mental radio, and a magic lasso. Although Wonder Woman was super strong, she did have one weakness: If a man ever attached chains to her bracelets, she would lose her strength.

The Lasso of Truth

In *Sensation Comics* #6, Wonder Woman was given an amazing accessory: an unbreakable magic lasso. The lasso was used to force others to obey Wonder Woman's every command. She would sometimes order someone to tell the truth, but she also used the lasso to force her captors to surrender, sing, dance, or stand on their heads. It wasn't until 1987 that it officially became known as the Lasso of Truth, with the sole power to force others to tell the truth.

Wonder Woman was now appearing in four different comic books and had her own newspaper comic strip. She had become the most popular female super hero in comics.

Fearsome Foes

Some of Wonder Woman's most memorable villains first appeared in her earliest adventures.

- Mars was the god of war, who grew stronger as men waged war on Earth.
- The Cheetah was a wealthy woman named Priscilla Rich, who wore a fur costume and became a criminal.
- Giganta was originally a giant ape that evolved into a tall, super-strong red-haired woman.
- Circe was a powerful witch who had been plotting against the Amazons for centuries.
- Doctor Poison was a Nazi spy who specialized in chemical weapons.

CHAPTER 6
Challenges

Wonder Woman was a success, but not everyone was pleased with the comic. Critics wrote letters to Max, complaining about her skimpy costume and the violence in her stories. A group of Catholic bishops formed a committee called the National Organization for Decent Literature and came up with a "Code for Clean Reading." They soon put Wonder Woman on a list of comics that were not recommended for children.

One bishop on the committee wrote to Max: "Practically the only reason for which 'Sensation Comics' was placed on the banned list of the N.O.D.L. was that it violates Point Four of the Code. Wonder Woman is not sufficiently dressed."

Max decided to ignore the critics. Wonder Woman's comics were among the top sellers of the time. And Max had a new idea for his latest super hero. He was thinking of having Wonder Woman join the all-male super hero team known as the Justice Society of America in *All-Star Comics*.

In 1942, Max included a one-page poll in *All-Star Comics* #11 that asked readers this question: "Should WONDER WOMAN be allowed, even though a woman, to become a member of the Justice Society?" After the first 1,801 questionnaires were returned, Max reported that 1,265 boys and 333 girls had voted "Yes." Only 197 boys and 6 girls had voted "No."

Wonder Woman joined the Justice Society in *All-Star Comics* #12 in a story written by Gardner Fox. It was the first Wonder Woman story not written by Bill, and it was also a major disappointment to him. In that story, Wonder Woman was made the group's secretary! In the stories that followed, the male heroes would head out to save the day while Wonder Woman stayed behind to keep the notes.

"Unfortunately, as secretary and honorary member, I have to remain behind," she explained to her teammates in *All-Star Comics* #14. "But I'll be with you in spirit!"

In another Justice Society adventure a few issues later, the story opened with Wonder Woman declaring, "Gentlemen! The minutes of all past Justice Society meetings have been *stolen*!"

Hawkman asked, "Are you sure you didn't take the record book home to type up the latest minutes?"

"Absolutely!" replied Wonder Woman. "But just to be on the safe side I'll go home and check on it."

After that, she departed and never returned for the rest of the fifty-page story.

Bill's own Wonder Woman stories, however, continued to champion women's rights. In one tale, Wonder Woman came to the aid of women working at a department store who were underpaid. Some had even been fired by the store's wealthy owner after they went on strike. At the end of the story, the owner announced, "Girls, starting now your salaries are doubled!"

Gardner Fox and Bill Marston clearly had very different ideas about the role of a female super hero.

Wonder Women of History

In 1942, a monthly feature was added to the *Wonder Woman* comic books: four-page biographies called "Wonder Women of History." They were initially written by Alice Marble, who was the top women's tennis champion in the world. Each new story celebrated a real-life "wonder woman," including Florence Nightingale, Marie Curie, Susan B. Anthony, and Helen Keller. By the time the feature ended in 1954, the lives of more than seventy-five notable women had been profiled.

CHAPTER 7
Hard Times for Heroes

Bill Marston died from cancer on May 2, 1947, just one week before his fifty-fourth birthday. He had written or supervised nearly every Wonder Woman script since her first appearance in 1941. He was working on a Wonder Woman story two days before he died.

Super hero comic books were becoming less popular in the decade after World War II. Perhaps costumed heroes seemed less important now that the world was at peace. Sales of super hero comics began to fall, and many titles were canceled. Superman, Batman, and Wonder Woman were among the few who managed to survive. The rest of the Justice Society all quietly disappeared.

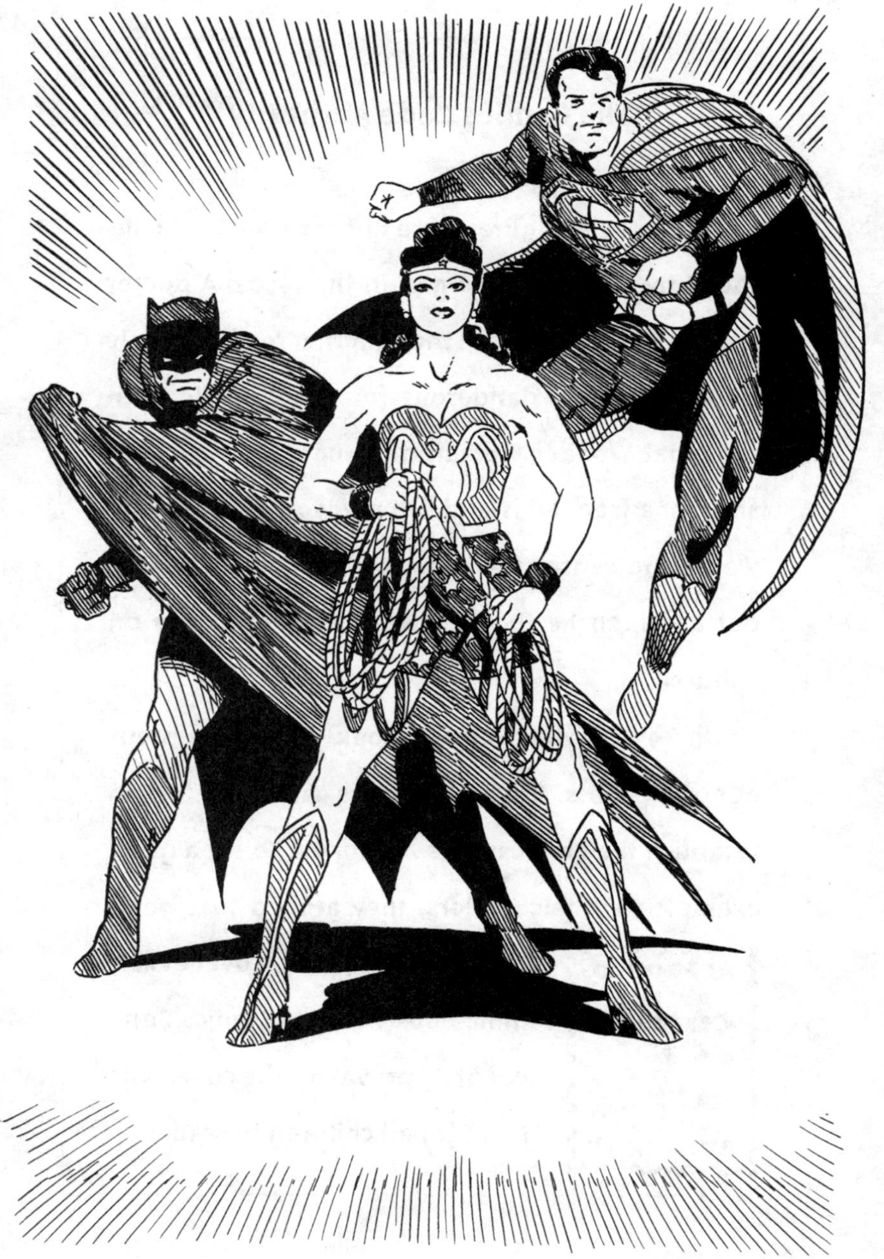

The Comics Code Authority

Lower sales figures were not the only problems faced by super hero comics in the 1950s. A doctor named Fredric Wertham thought that reading comic books could be dangerous for children. He even said that Wonder Woman must hate men because she came from an island of only women! Wertham wanted to censor the comics, which meant taking out anything he thought was a bad influence on children.

In 1954, fifteen comic book publishers went out of business. Other publishers came together to establish the Comics Code Authority. To set a good example for their readers, they agreed that good  would always triumph over evil. A comic book with the Comics Code Seal of Approval on the cover was "safe" for all children to read.

With fewer super heroes in comic books, romance comics suddenly became very popular with kids, and DC decided that Wonder Woman needed more romance in her life. Wonder Woman continued her super hero's mission, but it was becoming increasingly clear that what she *really* wanted was to settle down with her boyfriend, Steve Trevor. She started writing a newspaper advice column, offering tips to girls on how to find love. In other stories, she was a babysitter, a movie actress, and a fashion model. The cover of *Sensation Comics* #94 portrayed Wonder Woman as weak and helpless as she was carried in the arms of Steve Trevor. Even her famous red boots were replaced

with yellow ballet slippers. When the "Wonder Women of History" feature was canceled, it was replaced by articles with titles such as "Wedding Forecast" and "Strange Romantic Beliefs!"

The strongest and wisest of the Amazons seemed to have lost some of her true power.

CHAPTER 8
Wonder Woman Triumphant

By the 1960s, super hero comics were making a comeback. Wonder Woman became a founding member of a new super hero team called the Justice League of America. Some of DC's top heroes, including Superman, Batman, Green Lantern, and Aquaman, formed a new team, and Wonder Woman took her place as a full-fledged—and *active*—member.

At this same time, a new movement for women's rights started gaining strength. A group called the National Organization for Women was founded in 1966. With a focus on fighting for equal pay and equal rights, the movement came to be known as women's liberation.

Just as this was happening, though, Wonder

Woman took a step backward and lost her superpowers. Although Wonder Woman was now part of the Justice League, her own comic books were not selling very well. DC decided that drastic changes were in order. The company decided to change everything about Wonder Woman except her name.

The "new" Wonder Woman made her debut in 1968. She was still named Diana, but she no longer had superpowers or her famous red, white, and blue uniform. Instead, she owned a dress shop, wore stylish fashions, and worked as an international spy. The Amazons, Paradise Island, and even Steve Trevor were all written out of the story.

The first issue of the "new" *Wonder Woman*, 1968

Dennis O'Neil, the writer of the new stories, explained, "I saw it as taking a woman and making her independent, and not dependent on superpowers. I saw it as making her thoroughly human and then an achiever on top of that, which, according to my mind, was very much in keeping with the feminist agenda."

The goal—sometimes called their *agenda*—of people who are feminists is to establish equality between men and women. They work to make sure that educational and professional opportunities for women are equal to those for men.

One world-famous feminist named Gloria Steinem had grown up reading Wonder Woman comics in the 1940s and had fallen in love with the character as Bill Marston had written her. She did *not* approve of the "new" Wonder Woman.

Gloria said, "By 1968 she had given up her magic lasso, her bracelets, her invisible plane, and all her superhuman Amazonian powers. She had become Diana Prince, a mere mortal who walked about in boutique clothes. It was in this sad state that I first rediscovered my Amazon super hero in 1972."

Gloria Steinem

Gloria Steinem is an American journalist, political activist, and feminist organizer. She cofounded *Ms.* magazine in 1972. Instead of the recipes and decorating tips found in most women's magazines of the time, *Ms.* featured stories on the fight for women's rights.

"I realized as a journalist that there really was nothing for women to read that was controlled by women, and this caused me, along with a number of other women, to start *Ms.* magazine," said Gloria.

Today, Gloria travels the world as a spokeswoman on issues of equality. And *Ms.* magazine is still going strong more than forty-five years after its first issue.

Gloria decided to rescue Wonder Woman and convinced DC Comics to allow her to put Wonder Woman—wearing her original costume—on the cover of the first regular issue of *Ms.* magazine in 1972. A story in the magazine called upon DC to restore Wonder Woman's former superpowers.

Soon after that, DC announced that the original Wonder Woman would return.

Gloria reported that she "got a call from one of Wonder Woman's tougher male editors. 'Okay,'

he said. 'She's got all her Amazon powers back.
She talks to the Amazons on Paradise Island. Now
will you leave me alone?'"

"I said I would" was Gloria's reply.

With the return of her costume and her
superpowers, Wonder Woman was ready to make
her biggest move yet, conquering the world of
television.

In 1973, she joined forces with the DC heroes
Superman, Batman and Robin, and Aquaman
in the *Super Friends* animated television series.

Three new characters were also created for the show: Wonder Dog and a girl and boy named Wendy and Marvin.

Super Friends made its debut as part of ABC's Saturday morning cartoon lineup, and it was a big hit with kids. New episodes were produced until 1986 and then rerun for decades after that. Along the way, Wendy and Marvin and Wonder Dog were dropped from the show. They were replaced by the Wonder Twins: Zan and Jayna, and their blue monkey from outer space, Gleek.

Many episodes of the show began with the heroes gathered together in their official headquarters, known as the Hall of Justice. The giant TroubAlert computer would reveal a problem somewhere on Earth or in outer space.

The heroes would work together to save the day and find time to protect Wendy, Marvin, and the Wonder Twins from harm.

Even a few of Wonder Woman's most famous opponents appeared on the show, including the Cheetah and Giganta. And although Wonder Woman had the power to fly, she usually chose to pilot her Invisible Jet.

Voices of Wonder Woman

Over the years, many women have provided a voice for the character of Wonder Woman. Actress Shannon Farnon was the voice of the Amazing Amazon on the *Super Friends* cartoons for over a decade. Susan Eisenberg voiced Wonder Woman even longer, performing for over seventeen years in dozens of video games and animated cartoons.

Lucy Lawless, who became famous on TV as an Amazonian warrior on *Xena: Warrior Princess*, was the voice actress for the 2008 cartoon *Justice League: The New Frontier.*

Susan Eisenberg, Shannon Farnon, and Lucy Lawless (front)

In 1976, a new Wonder Woman television show was introduced. Actress Lynda Carter brought the character to life, and for the next three years she helped transform Wonder Woman from a comic book super hero to a worldwide superstar. For decades after the show went off the air, Lynda Carter remained the ideal symbol of Wonder Woman for many fans of the character.

The first season of the *Wonder Woman* TV series was set during World War II, and it closely followed Bill Marston's original stories. Steve Trevor was a pilot, and Diana Prince was his secretary. Whenever there was danger, Diana Prince would start spinning around, faster and faster, until she magically transformed into Wonder Woman.

According to Lynda, the spin was her idea. "In the comic book, Diana Prince just left and came back," she said. "But for the show, they couldn't figure out how to make the change." Because Lynda was a trained dancer, she knew that she could do an impressive spin to make the transformation.

One character on the TV series did not appear in Marston's stories but was instead introduced in a 1969 comic book. That was Wonder Woman's younger sister Drusilla, also known as Wonder Girl. She was played on the show by actress Debra Winger, and she could spin almost as fast as Lynda Carter.

Seasons two and three of the show featured some major changes, including a different network and a title change to *The New Adventures of Wonder Woman*. The setting was changed from the 1940s to the 1970s. Lynda Carter continued as Wonder Woman, but she was now partnered

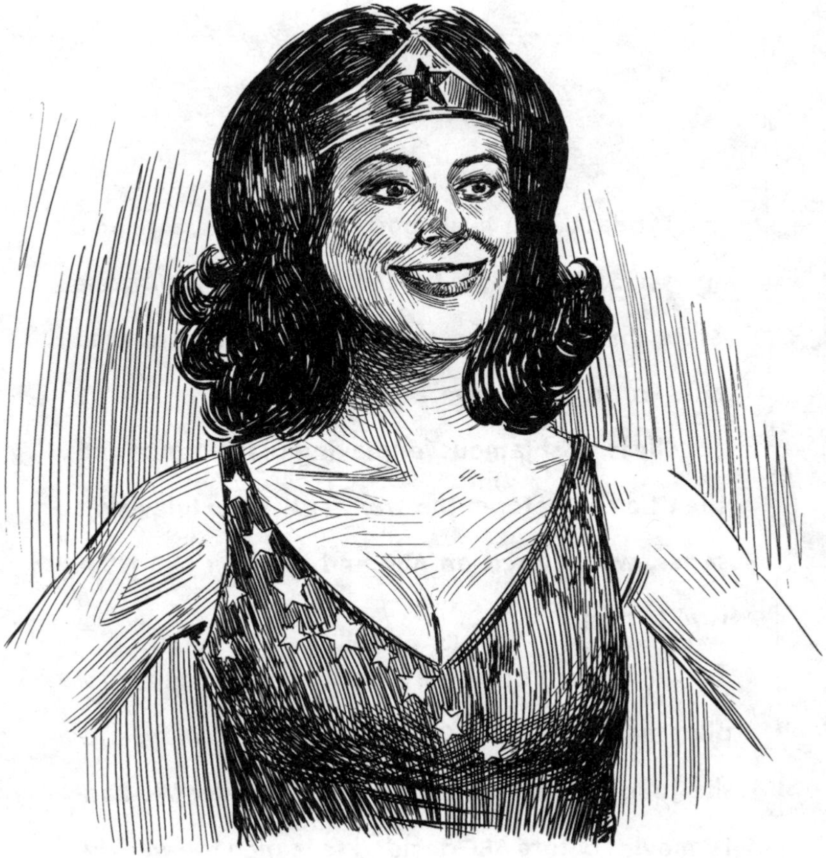

Debra Winger as Wonder Girl

with Steve Trevor's son. Instead of fighting Nazis, Wonder Woman now worked as an agent for a government organization battling criminals on Earth and aliens from outer space.

Lynda Carter

Lynda Carter was born in Phoenix, Arizona, in 1951. She was voted "most talented" at Arizona State University, and she went on to be crowned Miss World USA in 1972.

She is most famous for playing Diana Prince and the title character in the *Wonder Woman* television series, which aired on ABC and later on CBS from 1976 to 1979.

Lynda Carter first played the role in the 1975 TV pilot movie *The New, Original Wonder Woman*, and she followed that with two more Wonder Woman TV movies before ABC decided to launch the weekly series.

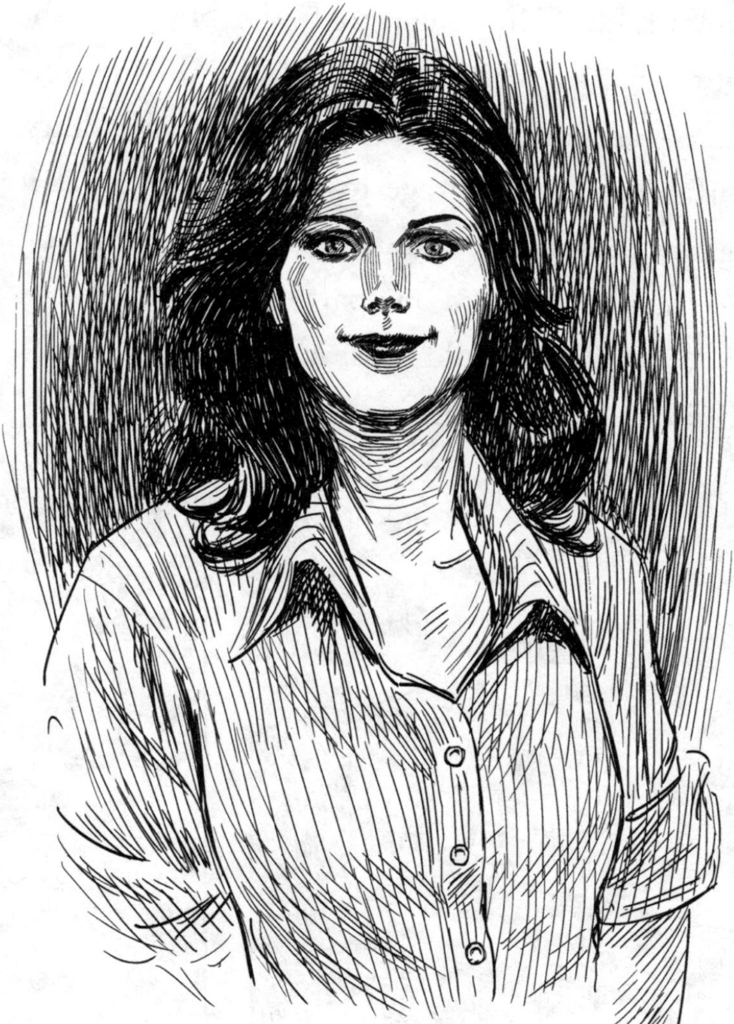

Trying to explain Wonder Woman's appeal, Lynda said, "The magic tools she brings to the fight—the bracelets, the lasso, the invisible plane—are only as good as her own ability, confidence, and courage to wield them. In that regard, perhaps she is not so different from you and me. We all share one part of ourselves to the world, while we hold close the ultimate power within us. Only when we trust in ourselves do we reach our fullest potential."

After the success of the live-action TV series, a flood of Wonder Woman merchandise hit the stores, including dolls, lunch boxes, cookie jars, and even Halloween costumes.

"There were those who refused to leave their TV sets on Wonder Woman night," said Gloria Steinem. "A few young boys even began to dress up as Wonder Woman on Halloween—a true revolution."

CHAPTER 9
Wonder Woman Goes to the Movies

After the *Wonder Woman* TV show ended in 1979, the character continued to change in comic books. Over the decades, many felt that the stories of Wonder Woman and several other DC characters had grown too complicated. It was difficult for new readers to fully understand them. In 1985, DC decided to simplify matters, and nearly every character was altered by a huge event known as "Crisis on Infinite Earths." It was a sort of time warp that allowed the characters to start over. There were new origin stories for many of the heroes, including Wonder Woman.

Writer and artist George Pérez, who took over the *Wonder Woman* comic book, had a plan to "stick to Greek mythology." In addition to adding

CRISIS *on infinite earths*

DEATH AT THE DAWN OF TIME!

MARV WOLFMAN · GEORGE PEREZ & JERRY ORDWAY · JOHN COSTANZA · ANTHONY TOLLIN
WRITER / EDITOR · ARTISTS · LETTERER · COLORIST

BRAINIAC IS DESTROYED...

NOW PSIMON SAYS LUTHOR MUST DIE AS WELL!

YOU TWO REALLY HAD A SCHEME GOING THERE, DIDN'T YOU? NOT NICE, LUTHOR... NOT NICE AT ALL!

RECRUITING ALL US SO-CALLED SUPER-VILLAINS...

...SENDING US TO TAKE OVER THREE OF THE EARTHS AND TO BATTLE THEIR MIGHTIEST HEROES...

...AND NO MATTER WHICH SIDE WON, YOU INTENDED TO PICK UP THE PIECES AND RULE BY YOURSELVES!

FORTUNATELY, I AM A RATHER SUSPICIOUS TYPE... I STAYED BEHIND AND OVERHEARD YOU.

SO NOW YOU WILL DIE WHILE I LET YOUR PLAN CONTINUE-- ONLY WITH ME IN CHARGE. SUCH A GOOD PLAN, LUTHOR.

PSIMON THANKS YOU FOR IT!

WHAT A SHAME YOU WON'T LIVE LONG ENOUGH TO ENJOY IT!

more Greek gods and goddesses, he changed the name of Paradise Island to Themyscira. He also took away the weakness that Wonder Woman would lose her powers if a man ever attached chains to her bracelets.

Over the years, several DC Comics characters—Superman, Batman, Supergirl, Green Lantern, and even the villainous Catwoman—had starred in their own big-budget movies. Some were very successful, especially the Superman and Batman movies.

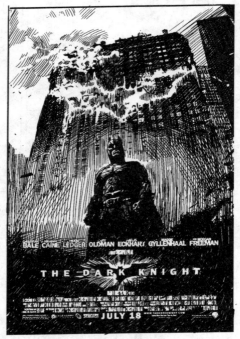

Wonder Woman had to wait for her chance to shine on the big screen. But it was worth it.

The first Wonder Woman to appear in the movies was a tiny plastic version of the character. That was the 3-D animated LEGO Wonder Woman, who showed up in *The LEGO Movie* in 2014. For the first time in movie theaters, Wonder Woman twirled her magic lasso and used her superpowers to beat up the bad guys.

But that was just the start of the Amazing Amazon's new career on-screen. In 2016, actress Gal Gadot became instantly popular when she portrayed Wonder Woman in the movie *Batman v Superman: Dawn of Justice*. The following year, she starred in the *Wonder Woman* feature film, one of the most successful movies of the year.

WONDER WOMAN

JUNE 2
SEE IT IN REAL D 3D AND IMAX 3D

That film's director, Patty Jenkins, said, "I watched the TV show, and she was everything a girl could aspire to be: strong and kind, exciting and stylish, powerful and effective, and just as fierce as the boys. I found that the Lynda Carter series was very, very true to the spirit of the original run of William Marston's *Wonder Woman*."

Patty Jenkins

Gal Gadot

Gal Gadot was born near Tel Aviv, Israel, in 1985, and was crowned as Miss Israel in 2004.

Gal began her acting career in 2007, playing the lead role in the Israeli TV series drama *Bubot*, which means "Dolls." She launched her movie career two years later in *Fast & Furious*. After that came roles in several movies, including *Knight and Day*, *Date Night*, and *Keeping Up with the Joneses*. But it was her performance as Wonder Woman that made her a star. Playing the role of the Amazing Amazon was a dream come true for Gal.

"What attracted me so much to this character is that she is so many different things, and they live within her in such a beautiful way," said Gal. "She's the greatest warrior in the comics, but she can also be vulnerable, sensitive, confident, and confused . . . everything, all at once. And she never

hides her intelligence or her emotions."

Gal Gadot won widespread acclaim for her portrayal of Wonder Woman in the 2017 blockbuster movie.

"What I cared about the most was trying to make a movie that was true to the character that has lasted for seventy-five years," said Patty. "But for many years I have been saying, 'There is a massive following of Wonder Woman.' And it was baffling to me that she, the biggest super hero in history, was not on-screen."

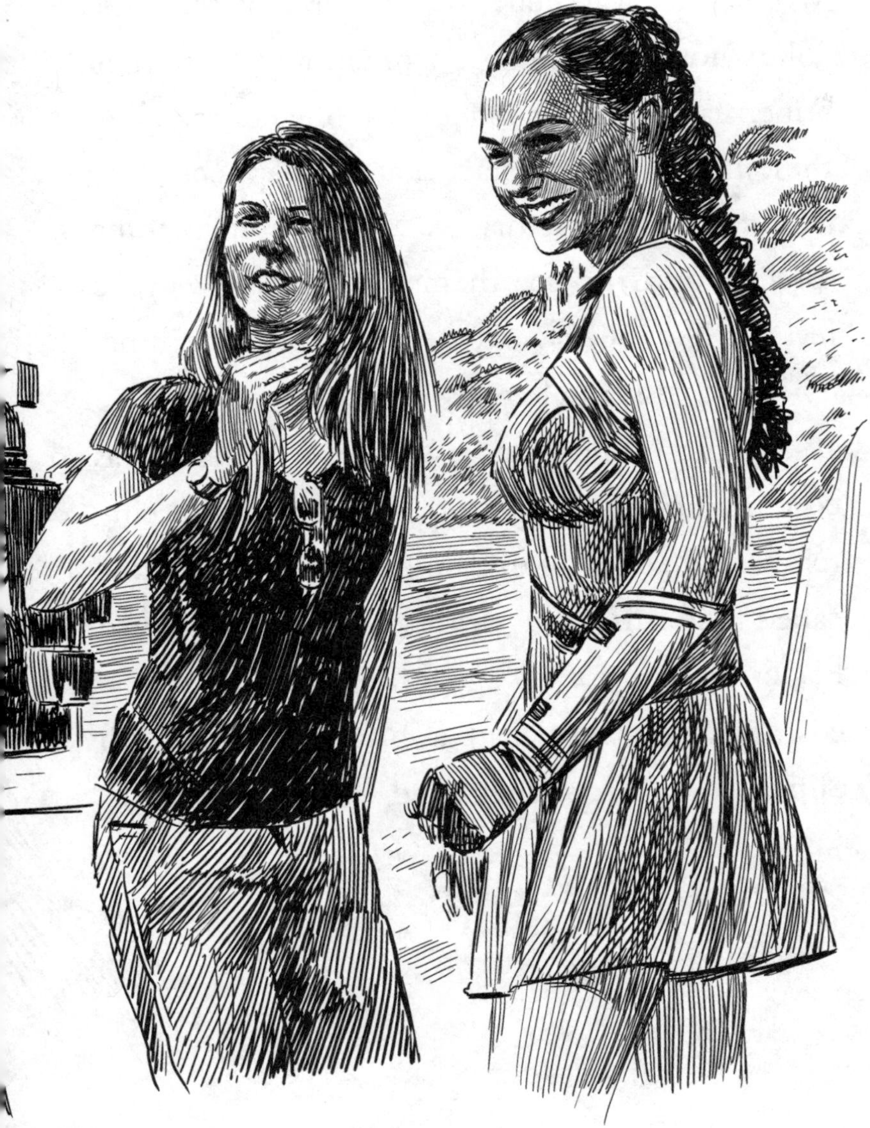

Speaking about the importance of Wonder Woman as a female super hero, Patty said, "She's not about being a woman any more than Superman's about being a man. She's doing all of these things, and the fact that she happens to be a woman is the victory. . . . What a great thing for little girls, to see themselves in that way, to feel not like they have to be a 'female' something. They can just be a hero."

At the same time Wonder Woman was conquering the big screen, she was being reinvented yet again in comic books in a storyline called "Rebirth." The writers and artists changed her origin story once again and gave her a new costume. She even had a brief romance with Superman before she reunited with Steve Trevor.

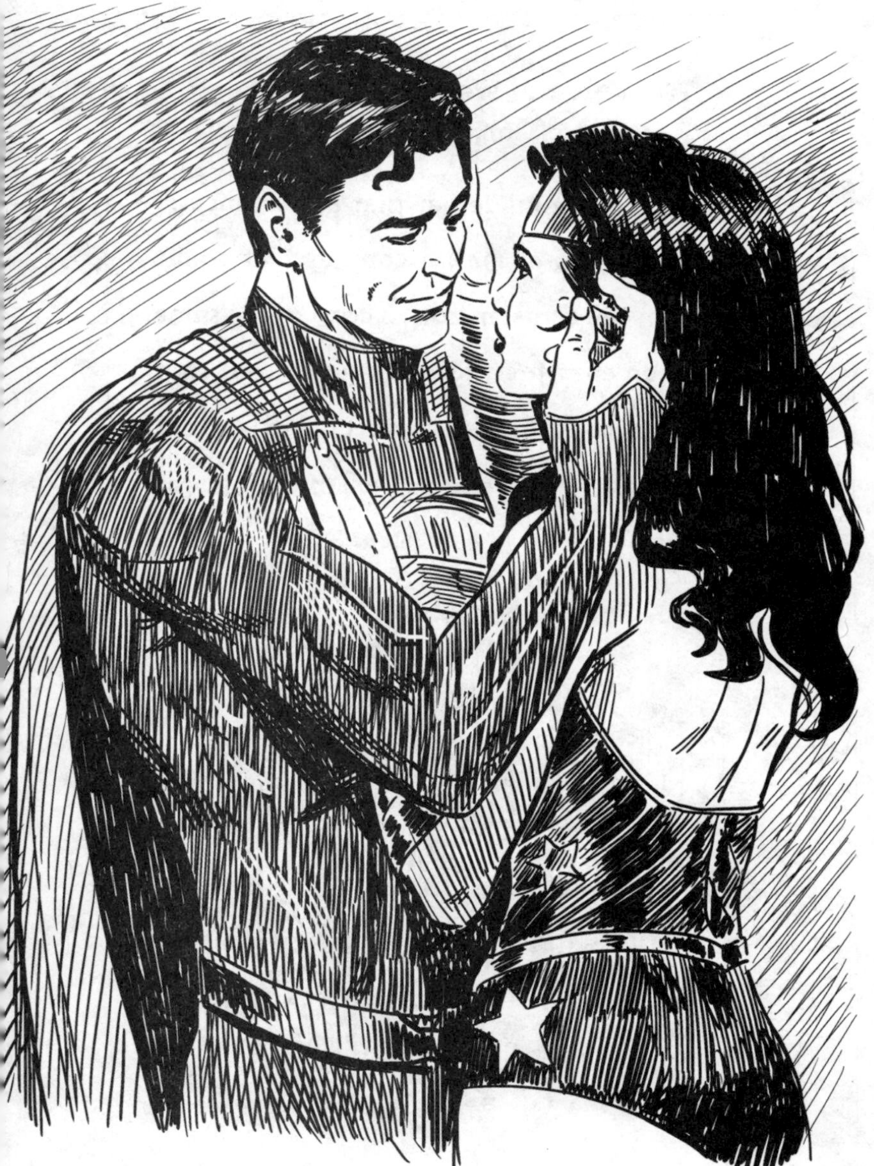

The Value of Wonder Woman

Wonder Woman made her first appearance in *All-Star Comics* #8. In 1941, a copy of that comic book sold for ten cents. In 2017, a copy of the same comic sold on eBay for a record $936,223.00! That same year, a copy of *Sensation Comics* #1 sold for $399,100.00, and *Wonder Woman* #1 sold for $226,877.77!

In 2016, Lynda Carter returned to the world of super heroes when she portrayed President Olivia Marsdin on the *Supergirl* TV show. Was her character's last name perhaps inspired by that of Wonder Woman's creator?

In 1941, Bill Marston was inspired by centuries-old Greek myths when he created Wonder Woman. Since then, her ongoing stories have entertained millions of readers and viewers. She has even become a symbol of the continuing fight by women for equal rights. She is more popular and more admired than ever before. She has truly earned the name "Wonder Woman" and has become the hero the world needs most.

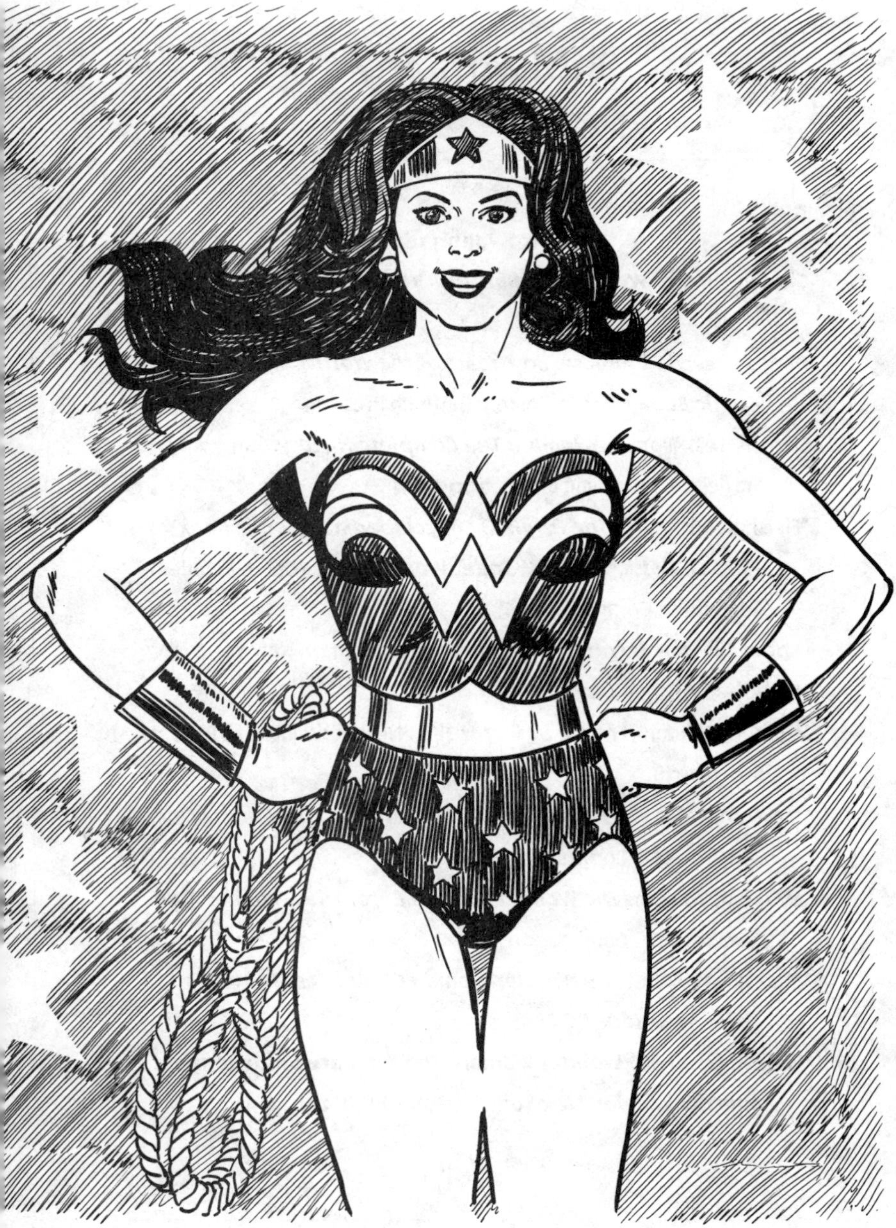

Bibliography

*Books for young readers

Chesler, Phyllis. *Wonder Woman.* New York: Holt, Rinehart and Winston, 1972.

Daniels, Les. *DC Comics: Sixty Years of the World's Favorite Comic Book Heroes.* Boston: Bulfinch Press, 1995.

Daniels, Les. *Wonder Woman: The Complete History.* San Francisco: Chronicle Books, 2000.

*Fleisher, Michael L. *The Original Encyclopedia of Comic Book Heroes, Volume Two: Wonder Woman.* New York: Macmillan Publishing Company, 1976.

Lepore, Jill. *The Secret History of Wonder Woman.* New York: Alfred A. Knopf, 2014.

Marston, William. *The Lie Detector Test.* New York: Richard R. Smith, 1938.

*Marston, William. *The Wonder Woman Chronicles, Volume One.* New York: DC Comics, 2010.

*Marston, William. *The Wonder Woman Chronicles, Volume Two.* New York: DC Comics, 2011.

*Marston, William. *The Wonder Woman Chronicles, Volume Three.* New York: DC Comics, 2012.

*Walker, Landry Q. *Wonder Woman: The Ultimate Guide to the Amazon Warrior.* New York: DK Publishing, 2017.